Two Men Fighting in a Landscape

Sept. 16, 2016

To Barry,
An old friend whose musicianship continues to amaze and inspire me.
— Bill Christophersen

Two Men Fighting in a Landscape

Poems by

Bill Christophersen

Kelsay Books

© 2015 Bill Christophersen. All rights reserved. This material may not be reproduced in any form, published, reprinted, recorded, performed, broadcast, rewritten or redistributed without the explicit permission of Bill Christophersen. All such actions are strictly prohibited by law.

Cover Art: Jock Pottle

ISBN 13: 978-0692495582

Kelsay Books
Aldrich Press
www.kelsaybooks.com

*For my father, George Christophersen (1911–2002),
who savored words*

Acknowledgments

The following poems have been previously published, sometimes in slightly altered versions, as indicated:

Antioch Review: "Strangers Frightened the Little Chihuahua"
Apalachee Review: "Bishop's Crook Lamppost"
Borderlands: "Night Scene"
Carolina Quarterly: "Flight Patterns"
Hanging Loose: "Crabbers" "Elegy for a Pencil" "Streetscape"
Light Quarterly: "An Essay on Pope" "Sermon on the Mount" "Meditation on a Quip by Frost"
Pudding Magazine: "Latino in a Landscape of Fire Escapes"
Right Hand Pointing: "Baker" "Engine" "Pheromones"
Sierra Nevada Review: "Veterans Cemetery: Corinth, Miss."
South Dakota Review: "The Bee-Loud Glade" "Westhampton Two-Step"
White Pelican Review: "Summons"

Contents

Acknowledgments

Old Movies

Picnic	13
Engine	16
Bronx Haiku	17
Bishop's Crook Lamppost	19
Night Scene	21
Grandma and Grandpa T. in a Prospect of Flowers	22
To A.S., Water Strider on the Academic Stream	26
"Youth Killed in $2 Mugging"	27
Old Movie	28
London on a Dollar a Day	36
Unnerved in Norway	37
Blues for Vinnie	38
Latino in a Landscape of Fire Escapes	40
The Blackest Crow	41
Streetscape with Blazing Locusts	43

Walks of Life

Surfer	47
Baker	49
Crabbers	50
Ironworkers	52
Fisher	53
Wag	54
Veteran	55
Treasurers	56
Copy Editors	58
Harrier	59
Poet	61

Flight Patterns

Flight Patterns	65
Summons	67
Pheromones	68
Westhampton Two-Step	69
Elegy for a Pencil	70
My Father's Pills	72
Broken Record	75
Veterans Cemetery: Corinth, Miss.	76

Two Men Fighting in a Landscape

The Anxiety of Influence	79
Anecdote of a Bar	80
Ajar in Tennessee	81
Strangers Frightened the Little Chihuahua	83
Meditation on a Quip by Frost	84
Windstorm	85
Sermon on the Mount	86
Composed Upon the George Washington Bridge	88
An Essay on Pope	89
In the Pines	90
A Malediction for Bidding, "'Morning!"	91
Off the Fashion Police	93
For Galway Kinnell	94
Confections of a Hooligan	97
The Bee-Loud Glade	99
God Has 99 Names (and an Unlisted Number)	101
The Take-Away	102
Two Men Fighting in a Landscape	105

The Wanderer

The Wanderer	109

Notes
About the Author

Old Movies

Picnic

Half a century removed from the cloudless sky that gave
birth to a glimmer that grew louder by degrees and finally
threatened to kill me one Saturday in 1953, I
remember this: The movie of my life was screening
in my four-year-old head as I sprawled in a twilight zone
of waving dandelions and horizontal grass in the nearly
treeless expanse of Ferry Point Park in the Bronx, the
Long Island Sound a stone's throw away, lapping
at the rocks I'd spent the morning playing on.

I had finished the drumstick, the slice of watermelon, the
Ritz crackers, the thermos of cream soda; had left
the island that was our picnic blanket, walked away
from that after-lunch scene grown tiresome as Mom
fed the baby and Dad dozed on one elbow; had gone
to have a run, a look around, to kick the tops off some
milkweeds, pull some grass up by the roots, roust a
seagull. The lop-lop of a helicopter registering, I
looked up and pinpointed it, a brilliant

sliver in the afternoon sky. I raced its gleam, my
ankles wreaking havoc with the milkweed but
my handicap eaten up in no time by the
copter, louder now and bigger, its
rotors' blur darkening as it gained, its
runners plainly visible, the race a genuine
contest now as the thing swooped low, ear-
splittingly low, then stopped overhead and started
getting larger. It dawned on me that the copter,

whose pilot would not see me, was preparing
to land. Panicking, I tripped and

fell, face forward, the spiked grass bending
back around me. Above, the copter—
a clear bubble, two men visible—
rocked from side to side in the heavy
air, its gale pressing me down, my
legs gone rubber, cries inaudible,
Mom, Dad too far away to help.

If you've ever feared for your life, you know
what people say is true: The past fast-forwards,
flashes by, a streaming video of reruns.
I closed my eyes, covered my ears and
watched the ill-timed movie. Overhead,
the noise changed pitch. I looked: The grass
was upright again, the copter flying backward
into the sky. My crying audible now, my
father, shirttails flying, fetched me up.

     * * *

> *green night-light pop's harmonica*
> *bury me not on the lone prairie &*
> *nickels zigzag in the glass machine*
> *but the zebra's head on the barn is*
> *screaming a long thin man with*
> *mustard teeth spits melon pits &*
> *grandma's high-button shoes dead*
> *foxes draped around her shoulders &*
> *the sandlot soda shack wolf leaps but*
> *it's on a chain & teenagers in t-shirts*
> *fight on the handball court we eat*
> *ritz crackers on a slanted rock &*

*the radio plays put another nickel in
the nickelodeon sister climbing the
wall the nurse from 7G at midnight
trash men sling ash cans checkered
taxis pass the five & dime grandma
trills mockingbird hill as big leaves
blow like hands across a broken
sidewalk & we eat a sugar cruller in
horn & hardart while a steam shovel
digs up pieces of street & the toaster
whose sides fold down catches fire
two dolphins spout fountains of water
over pennies goldfish purple houses
cover the dolphins & a forest plays
we three kings & floorboards creak
in the toy store where a rumpled clerk
climbs a ladder on wheels for a silver
axe & a freight train goes in one side
of a mountain & comes out the other*

               *   *   *

So the film unspooled, whirring, then
yielded abruptly to sunlight, memory
having made its flash documentary.
I've never seen the like again and
don't know (much less want to know)
how it ends. But I know that death's
a rotary blade trolling a cloudless sky, a
glass insect hovering then homing in, a
jealous god overflying a family picnic.

Engine

Its miniature cowcatcher catches my eye
from the bottom of a shoebox full of gimcracks
and old Polaroids: a gilt locomotive,
crisply detailed from camshaft to smokestack,
an inch or so long. I scrutinize the black
hole of its window.
                        It's 1955.
My four-year-old sister and I are walking back
from Sunday school. We stop outside the dry
cleaner's, try the charm machine, and right
away her dumb-luck penny wins this prize.
Later I would pester her to swap
the charm she loved. She would refuse and cry.
I would persist, bull-headed, till it was mine.
For a cheesy, dime-a-dozen bubble pipe.

Bronx Haiku

View from flat: brick wall,
alley, slice of street and sky,
rooftop with beach chairs.

Stickball game on hold:
Kids play in the flash flood of
an open hydrant.

Roosevelt High School's
neoclassical facade.
Muscle shirts, ducktails.

Heat hunkers down. Bad
air—one long nicotine stain—
blankets the projects.

Straphangers dream cold
beers, frosted glasses; settle
for a cracked window.

Rush hour over, truck
horns die down on Tremont. Tock
of bongos on Mace.

Ten p.m. Young guys
church-key cans of Schlitz, bum smokes,
sing shoo-doo, doo-wah.

In streetlamp's spotlight,
wizened Cubans on milk crates
slap down dominoes.

Beyond the fire escape
the moon climbs—an orange lens
looking for tinder.

Bishop's Crook Lamppost

In my dream of the prewar
housing project in the Bronx
where I grew up, the bishop's crook
lamppost with the orange globe
is tilted slightly. It is night,
and St. Dominic's, which even
in the dream I know should be a
couple blocks north of the railroad
trestle, stands across the street.
So do the Italian girls in their
maroon and white uniforms. They
are out there waiting for the sun
to come up and school to open.
I'm standing at the bedroom
window, head spinning. In
the living room, Martin
Luther is chatting with my
folks, who want to play him the
Rosalie Sorrels record where she
yodels, but he's not listening. He's
demonstrating yo-yo tricks: walk
the dog, round the world, over the
falls, rock the cradle. He says we
need to master these tricks right
now, in case we're called upon
to vindicate our faith publicly by
performing them for the PTA.
He says let's start with this one
where we make the yo-yo sleep.
When I hear how serious he sounds,
I forget about trestles and my

parents' phonograph, start
thinking about the lamppost,
which is tilting noticeably now,
just as I am tilting toward the
Giants, the Catholic girls,
the Five Satins: sins
that won't go over well
in the neighborhood.

Night Scene

Dinner was beans and pasta and boring talk
of a severance package. Excused, we hit our homework.
You drank your coffee, had a smoke. And then,
instead of your accounts portfolio, took down
a sheet of something black resembling
oak tag and a scraping tool, and began to scrape
white lines and spaces on the oak tag's night.
We multiplied percentages from pie charts.
You scraped a field of snow, a house hip-deep
in drifts; a moon sliced by the wizard branches
of a tree. We fixed our own milk and cookies.
You moistened a brush in the Flintstones water glass,
painted the moon blue, the windows' tiny rectangles
red. We stood, then, toothbrushes in hand,
spellbound by the blizzard's aftermath, the birdlike
eyes of the house, the white, unsettling night.

Grandma and Grandpa T. in a Prospect of Flowers

*Raise the plastic gimcrack to the
light and squint: There they are,
fresh from church. She wears a fur
stole, a hat with netting; he, a gray
suit and gold-rimmed specs. Flowers
bloom in Kodachrome behind them.*

*

He raised collies, owned a
car with running boards. Wore woolen
long johns even in summer. Wouldn't
hear of air conditioning. Figured
sums in his head, drank Red Rose
tea and went to bed early, company
or no. Once the neighbor raked up a
hornets' nest. He pulled off his shirt,
waded into the fight.

*

He'd get up at six, sit
in the rocker, turn on
the lamp with the amber
shade and read his Bible
If you were quiet, you could
watch him read, the
rocker not rocking, sunlight
sneaking into the room
inch by inch.

*

The day after he died, we
went to be with Grandma in her
spotless house. After lunch I
played myself at checkers, flipped
Davy Crockett cards in the foyer.
Then I left the house, angled through
woods to the brook. It
wasn't moving. I
stood on the plank-and-rail
bridge looking for snakes. The
heat started getting to me.
Mosquitoes. Mud daubers.
Dragonflies. The air
was full of trouble.

*

When Grandma came to live with us,
Dad and I slept in the living room, stayed
up late watching "M Squad," "The Ten O'Clock News."
Grandma was like Chinese food—sweet and sour.
Sometimes at supper she would grumble,
tell me I was spoiled and should eat what
was put in front of me. She had a way
of filching my best potato chips. One night,
floating around in her white nightgown,
she decided to comb out her bun.
Came in and scared the piss out of me.

*

She was living with us because she'd
gotten nervous. When she was home
she was frightened by the lights that swept
her house at night—lights that were probably
cars turning the corner but that she thought
were flashlights. She watched too much
television. When Charles Van Doren
turned out to be a fraud, she took it
personally. Her hands, parched as old
lampshade, started shaking all the time.

*

Eventually Grandma wanted to be
back in her own house. There she
started thinking, I guess, about the
past and present, and there
couldn't have been much of a
comparison. One day she
locked the basement door behind her and
hung herself like a rucksack from a rafter.

*

"I'm a burden, Isabel," she had
said one night while I was doing
percentages and Mom was
emptying the washer. "I'm an old
woman whose day is past. I'm
no good to anyone anymore."

                              "That's
not true, Grandma," I had said, my words
four grains of sugar in a pot of oatmeal.

                *

*Like bees in October, they are
drawn to windows. Sometimes
they move—stale odors—
through our rooms. They
eye us vaguely or suspiciously,
look through us as through
gauze curtains. They understand
some things perfectly. Time
lives in them as in a building
with a doorman. When they
go, they take the keys but
leave the keychain ornament
in which their likenesses
smile in 3-D, incongruous,
in a prospect of flowers.*

To A.S., Water Strider on the Academic Stream

Old flake, old lunatic! What's become of you,
who turned AP Biology into a gag show?
Your cartoons featuring jet-lagged trilobites,
the fruit flies Arthropod and Hymenoptera,
the cosmic superhero Java Man,
and Professor Mandible, author of *Rogue Peptides*
and *Refuting the Krebs Cycle*, made the rounds
like samizdats. I can still see Mr. Gottlieb—
the fetal pig you dissected with celebrity-
chef panache, chatting the while to the carcass
("Mr. Gottlieb, stop looking so disgruntled . . .").
Your encore? Blowing off the Board exam.
("Employing diagrams, discuss how plants evolved."
 You sketched a cloud-veiled arm: "The Hand of God.")

"Youth Killed in $2 Mugging"

We moved a mattress together,
couple months back. Gawky
kid in red high-tops, used to
draw stuff in pen on the white parts.
Wannabe mustache. Three Stooges
sense of humor. Laughed a little
too much, you know? Laughed
with his whole body, like a
cartoon of somebody laughing. . . .
Shot Friday night. Crotona Park.
Two bucks on him. That's
subway fare plus, what, a
pack of Chiclets? And Bobby,
the cat was with him? Not a
scratch, no shit. Hasn't slept
for five days. He's walking
into walls, falling down stairs.
The super's wife, Mrs. Burgos,
she used to live around there,
Tremont and Crotona. Says the
women carry knives to church.

Old Movie

In the film noir that is my aggregated love life,
my most cinematic breakup is neither the midnight
screamfest on Broadway with the polymath nor the
rapprochement with the coed from California that
transmogrified into a revenge melodrama involving
her roommate's boyfriend. It isn't even the messy
parting of the ways with the academic secretary
who wanted me to don creased trousers and spank her.
Rather, it's the one whose mise en scène is Flushing

Meadow, where the 1964 World's Fair
left behind two towering, inscrutable
o*bjets* in the shape of golf tees and, nearby,
a giant aluminum-and-air replica of Earth,
poised on its rakish axis—a lopsided
golf ball waiting for God to drive it down the fairway.
We strolled across the plain of unpeopled grass,
she sketching plans for graduate work in special ed,
plans with which my ambitions as a street fiddler

were, she intimated, a dubious fit.
Margot! You turncoat! Though I'd be a fool to deny
you had a point. Still, to think that in the shadow
of all that incongruous hardware you sent me packing—
you, with your wire-rimmed glasses, who had worn
an orange long-underwear top and Moroccan sandals
on our first date, a game of (natch!) Careers. . . .
By then, of course, you'd had it up to here with me
for acing the exams I hadn't had time to study for;

embarrassing you by bodysurfing a shopping cart
down the produce aisle at Shoprite; waxing morose
at your perky wine-and-cheese soirée; and not even trying

to impress your suitemate, the one you said subscribed
to *TV Guide*. . . . In short, for being too devil-may-care
and not devil-may-care enough. (All right, I'll admit
this one-sided account is as defensive and self-serving
as your reason for cutting me loose was unpersuasive.
In spinning this tale, I've already spun our characters;

made mine not more endearing but at least a tad
less insecure and sophomoric. For the record,
I was both. And you? It's a cinch you weren't the one
I'd imagined you to be, much less that other one
I'd imagined you to be way back in high school,
when you first unhinged me with your sidelong pout.
Who were you? You who seemed, that day in Flushing,
to be inhabited by an alien pod?) Such bourgeois
airs! Don't say you don't remember

the December night I hitchhiked up to see you
in the horizontal snow: The car that picked me up
was all over the road. I arrived completely wired.
We went to a party that was mostly married couples
and cigarette smoke; left early; walked to your apartment,
mittened hand in gloved hand, and then bare hands
in army jacket pocket; stretched our limbs
on your Oriental rug, a cranberry-scented
candle burning, James Taylor's "Sweet Baby James"

on the stereo. . . . Remember? Me neither. Jeez, Louise,
how trite the recap sounds. Let's skip the period
seduction, rewind to the preliminary rushes
from eleventh grade (those adolescent cameos
won't double-cross us, eh?): Here's one of you

locking eyes with me in chem class, smiling—then
being transferred. . . . some kind of programming glitch.
Here's another one: you applying to be secretary
of the cross-country and track team (That can't be right:

what would we have wanted with a secretary?).
Twelfth-grade math class, then, where—hmm—you flirted
with the pommel-horse gymnast whose flat-top crew cut bristled
between us as my Boolean algebra heart
became the null set. . . . Hey: The period we spent
listening to *The Freewheelin' Bob Dylan* in the library,
earphones jacked into the same audio channel,
eyes averted, until the needle started skipping
on "Girl From the North Country" ("fair, fair, fair . . .").

That memory begins, at least, to testify
to what punched me up: your fine, unfussy hair,
for instance, and jackrabbit eyes; your unborrowed
laugh, your un-self-conscious slouch. . . . You were
farm-fresh in your peasant blouse; coltish
in your gangly legs and sorrel leotards;
even now I see you moving down the hall—
that quirky cross-country-skier's glide of a
walk you had, so different from the mincing

pliés of the other schoolgirls. But what was I
reading into your looks, your walk? Did they say
a blessed thing about your inner landscape? Isn't
every ponytail that tickles a young blade's peachfuzz
"different from all the rest"? Who exactly were you,
with your iridescent ballpoint pen? Did you resemble

even remotely the Mary Travers-cum-Marianne Faithfull
figment I projected in those disconcerting moments
when we scoped each other out in the cafeteria?

Yet I'd swear you *were* that unadulterated thing—
Never mind that I, with my Lutheran conscience,
was anything but the unpruned juniper
I imagined you to be; or that at 16
you hardly deserved gold stars on your report card
for being wispy-haired and winsome; never mind
that, for all I knew, you spent your downtime reading
Ayn Rand novels, Scientology tracts:
The you I saw—still see—was *sui generis.*

The homemade Christmas card (its colored foil
and masking tape simulating a stained-glass window)
cinched the matter: Who could conceive such a brilliant
handicraft except one equally brilliant, artlessly
brilliant, brilliant as foil, brilliant as a cathedral?
This meant I could go ahead and beat myself up
for my own pewter dullness; rationalize your every
cold shoulder, real or imagined, even as I
seethed beneath it; lacerate myself at will.

All the same, you surprised me with a letter
a month after graduation, saying that your summer
job in midtown stank but that one lunchtime
you'd found a sort of park that had been shoehorned
between two buildings—public benches extending
along a walkway beneath a glassed-in waterfall.
There you ate your carrots, read your Tolkein.

I was a camp counselor that summer. I don't
recall my reply, but do remember rereading

your letter (green ink, penmanship suggesting
strands of barbed wire) as if I were an infantryman
in a trench. Even bought myself a copy of
The Hobbit to be on your literary wavelength.
Later that year we met for coffee. The weather
was abominable. "Cold and rainy with a chance
of oobleck," you joked. You were smoking a cigarette,
wearing a chic overcoat and some kind of women's
department fragrance. I wasn't a bit amused.

I was in love, though, and stayed that way three years,
alternately working up courage and talking myself out
of the possibility that anything could ever come of it,
you being in Boston, me in New York. So when we
finally bit the bullet and got reacquainted,
I felt as if a nasty jigsaw puzzle I'd
been grumbling over for years had suddenly
assembled itself. Sure, I understood
that jigsaw puzzles are inherently unstable.

(So are continents, dynasties, saxophonists: The laws
of thermodynamics have it in for everything
that moves, you know? We're all bodies in motion
and, temporary force fields notwithstanding,
tend to remain that way.) Nevertheless,
here we had a situation where the marble
of Destiny had zigzagged waggishly across
the Chinese checkerboard, then come to rest
at the apex of the appointed triangle.

No two ways about it: That spring semester
we were in the zone. Lime rickeys. Vanilla crème
cookies. Darjeeling tea. Crossword puzzles.
That trippy project we got lost in in your kitchen,
that involved bending strands of copper wire,
then dipping them into jars of colored plastic
fluids that hardened in a transparent film. Your clock
with the hapless minute hand. The quaint way the Boston
subway had of shutting down at midnight. . . .

But even in the belly of contentment
there were gastrointestinal rumblings—jealousies;
mood swings; barbed retorts; infantile spats;
veiled criticisms; affectations; unilateral
declamations. The standard stuff, but how
was I to know? Math major that I almost became,
I thought if we were honest and watched our decimal points,
the arithmetic would take care of itself; the curve
of mutual want would continue to approach its asymptote.

Which it did, I suppose, although somewhere along the way,
English major that I was, I gave up trying
to graph its screwball path. The bottom line?
Love proved to be the domain of irrational numbers,
where perverse sequences repeat *ad nauseum*;
of imaginary numbers, where negative square roots
turn up in otherwise well-behaved equations—
jokers, as it were, among picture cards. . . .
Who'd have thought the language of the heart

would baffle worse than Northumbrian Middle English?
(Yet there it was, the sorry transliteration
staring me in the face: a blown midterm.)

I guess that by the time you wrote me off
you'd sorted out your feelings more than I,
whose head was full of bluegrass tunes, nostalgic
ballads about states I'd never been to.
I must have gotten over you, though, because
I spent that summer hitchhiking around the country.

We crave, I guess—film buffs that we are
during those excruciating years we later come to call
the best of our lives—to partake in a high-arc drama,
something grittier and grander than the run-of-the-mill
budget productions, spaghetti westerns and frantic,
humorless sitcoms that, even when we're young,
we sense we're bound to wind up in. How else to explain
our obsessive auditioning? We strut our stuff,
hoping, at least, to persuade ourselves we belong

in pictures, have what it takes to make
a little scene, something to set the gossip
columnists gossiping. (If we're lucky, we'll be able
to watch it with a modicum of embarrassment
later, when the relative entertainment value
of our lives has dwindled.) To be featured in the heart's
productions is to become a star, a legend in our
own minds: sultry, tempestuous, brooding,
the caricature of a self we scarcely know

co-starring with the caricature of another
we know even less about. It's babel—a virtual
ESL classroom, except that no one's here
to learn; we're here to emote, declaim, inflame;

to stoke a little fire that wants stoking;
generate a little buzz in the screening room,
where a hungry darkness quickens, even as the
uncut footage of our lives plays out
in broad daylight, amid bombastic props.

London on a Dollar a Day

for Sven Hagen

We were on the bum. You had a two-week's head
start when we met, and had got the basics down:
where to wash (tube restroom); how to make bread
taste like a meal (ketchup); how to earn a crown
(a shutterbug, you'd worked out an arrangement
with your hometown rag: you'd send them pics;
they'd wire enough to offset what you spent);
and—most important—where to find free digs
(Hyde Park; when it rained, a derelict tenement).
We lived like hobo royalty until one night,
asleep among planetrees near the Diana Fount,
we were rousted twice by bobbies between midnight
and two. "Enough," you said. We crossed a sward,
jumped a fence, slept tight in the park police's yard.

Unnerved in Norway

As the coastal road nears Troms—above the Arctic
Circle—it skirts a pinnacle of rock
that overlooks the rest (no mean trick,
as every way you look is chockablock
with white-capped peaks except directly down,
where a fjord's blue shoelace makes the altitude
real). I pulled into a turnaround,
then, under sway of an expansive mood,
resolved to climb the crest. The trek was slow.
I grew winded. It became a test of will.
I reached a shelf the wind had swept of snow,
and turned around. Mountains looked like hills.
I scanned the road, the fjord, the cloud-fleeced scree—
then froze, as the abyss looked into me.

Blues for Vinnie

for Chris Donald, a.k.a. Vinnie Taylor, 1949-1974

Gimlet-eyed; sardonic; often shit-faced;
affectless, sometimes; sometimes downright stupid
(the 40-odd parking tickets, many torn up,
all right there on the floor of your car the night
you ran the red light at 120th and Morningside
and got pulled over, so instead of T-ing you up
again, the cops impounded your car), you were
lightning in a bottle on the six-string,
deciphering not only the drop-tuned, 1930s
Delta stuff—Son House, Robert Johnson, Skip
James (whose panther-like howls and spidery
fingerings you, rallying, turned me on to
late one night at your place on 142nd
after I'd caught the cherry Country Gentleman
as it fell from your nodding hands, and fixed some tea
to keep you out of the zombie zone)—but also
the ornery ragtime stuff: Blind Blake's "Southern Rag,"
the Reverend Gary Davis's secular stuff,
one melody walking down the strings, the other
cross-dribbling up. And further back: the Scott
Joplin piano rags you resurrected,
their countermelodies unspooling, string-damped
and woodsmoked, from the beat-up Gemini II:
"Maple Leaf Rag," "Black and White Rag," "Magnetic Rag"—
gymnastic tunes you executed, high or hung over.
And then the higher-octane stuff: the electric
bottleneck blues—Muddy Waters, Elmore James;
Merle Travis's syncopated pattern-picking;
the Buck Owens / Don Rich '60s Bakersfield stuff;
the T-Bone Walker / Chuck Berry blues-and-boogie
solos that made the treble pickup sizzle. . . .

Thumb-style fandangos; rockabilly volleys
of notes that rose and swelled, your right hand going
wherever the crabbed or splayed left told it to.
Plugged in and lit—the way you liked to play—
you were a vintage Wurlitzer, a roadhouse
jukebox of 20th-century American music. . . .
That's the thing I thought about on hearing
you'd OD'd. Having put all that together,
why would you tempt the gods to confiscate it?

Latino in a Landscape of Fire Escapes

lips a cigarette, spit curl
imploding. All around:
empty lots,
projects, the
charred skulls of buildings.
Here, there,
T-shirts fly on clotheslines in the interstices.
In the foreground: bricks,
a gutted mattress, part
of a toilet. Water
trickles from an open hydrant.
His jacket zipper sticks.
The spit shine on his boot tops whistles.

The Blackest Crow

Barely awake, we stood piling instruments into the Impala.
The banjo protruded from the window;
the Dreadnought in its case was still on the roof.
We had to be onstage by noon.

The banjo—screw it—protruded from the window.
Fiddles in the trunk; ditto the tent, sleeping bags, backpacks.
We had to be onstage by noon.
You know how hilly Chappaqua is? How twisty the roads?

("The mandolin. . . ?" "In the trunk, with the backpacks.")
We tumbled in and headed out.
You know how hilly Chappaqua is? How twisty the roads?
We took it nice and slow

for ten minutes, heading out.
Someone was singing "The Blackest Crow,"
taking it nice and slow.
It's a ballad of faith and leave-taking.

Someone was singing "The Blackest Crow"
as we approached the entrance to the Taconic.
It's a ballad of leave-taking,
but we sat there, unable to catch a break in the traffic.

At the entrance to the Taconic
an unyielding line of cars sped by.
Seeing, at last, a might-could-risk-it break in traffic,
Dave made his move.

A line of cars, unyielding, had sped by
through most of "The Blackest Crow."
Then Dave made his move,
and as we accelerated into traffic, something went thud.

". . . Bright day will turn to night," someone sang,
and the engine coughed:
We accelerated into traffic, something went thud,
and the engine died.

As the engine coughed *(omigod)*,
the guitar we'd forgotten to stow fell from the roof,
hit the trunk. *And as it did, the engine died.*
Dave eased the car toward the shoulder.

(The guitar fell from the roof. . . . *And now?*
Pileup? Death in our wake? We its instrument?)
Dave eased the car onto the shoulder,
the Dreadnought in its case still riding the trunk.

"The blackest crow that ever flew
will surely turn to white.
If ever I prove false to you,
bright day will turn to night."

Streetscape with Blazing Locusts

The weather shifts again, a high-pressure system
displacing the acrid pall yesterday's thermal
inversion left squatting over Manhattan. It's
Halloween. I walk north along Morningside
from 110th, hood up, hands in pockets, taking in
the park, its cinder track, dog run and ramble
backed by miles of Harlem roofscape, remembering
the blood orange moon that floated above it all
one night last week, and the guy in a black windbreaker
who threw down on me—a 9mm semiautomatic—
in the hallway of my 121st Street apartment building
a year ago today. I'm still here, though, sporting
new front teeth to boot, their white, aligned
perfection belied on every side. The block's
still home, friends' entreaties notwithstanding—
never more so than on a day like this,
when a cold snap's set a match to the black locusts
and an electrical storm has left the pavement pod-strewn,
rain-glazed—a wash of gold and mango eclipsing
the tenements' sooty facades and that towering eyesore
of a dorm the university built on the lot above which
a prospect of sky used to stretch its oblong canvas.
So what if my northern exposure's gone south? So
what if tomorrow's attorneys wrangle nightly
over parking spots? It's the time of year when beauty
and vegetable death redeem incivility, unreason;
when old movies screen, uncut, on memory's laptop,
old legs vault park benches vicariously, and the
broken sidewalk squares of run-down side streets
mimic stained-glass windows for a couple of hours.

Walks of Life

Surfer

Finished with school, we loosed our tongues,
sang Beach Boys songs off-key, let time
go by (wasn't it relative, anyway?).
Our lives had reached a natural peak.
Car keys in hand, we had arrived. . . .
So what was all this talk about work?

None of us wanted to go to work,
get hitched. "Suited up?" we'd say, tongue
in cheek, to each other as we arrived
at the beach, and "Isn't it about time
you and that little fox, Miss Peek-
a-Boo, tied the knot?" ("What? No way!")

We liked to paddle out a ways
beyond the breakers, let the board do the work
of keeping us afloat as we scoped out a peak
among peaks worth turning the fiberglass tongue
around for. 'Be cool, it would arrive:
We'd take the drop, kick out in time

to avoid getting hammered ("cannonball time").
But the ocean has some gnarly ways.
You're drifting, dreaming, when a riptide arrives
out of nowhere. Now you've got your work
cut out. Got to focus, bite your tongue,
show some respect for the water's pique—

go with the counterflow, so to speak
("Don't fight your mamma"). In good time
you'll catch a break. . . . Or not: Your tongue

goes dry; you're treading water way
far out, board stripped away. . . . Better work
your butt back in before weather arrives,

you tell yourself. But weather's arriving
already, you see, as you snatch a peek
to windward. Is playing it cool gonna work?
Undertow's a mother; your window of time
is closing. Fight it? Let it have its way,
never mind the livid sky? . . . The tongue

that tastes fear savors time. Which, naturally, had its way
with us: We married, found work. Except one freestyler,
    who peeked
at the program and declined to arrive. Just surfed on, sticking
        out his tongue.

Baker

His confections, like your
brightest ideas, most
masochistic jealousies and
inveterate fears, bake
while you sleep, the off-white
braids inflating, the
currant-laden batter torqueing.
The baker yawns, lets them
rise, rolls out moist dough
for the next batch and
dreams a second.

Crabbers

Sometimes the bait in the traps outweighs the catch, says the
    mate, lighting his cigarette with a blowtorch.

Each trip it's something else, he says. Something hairy. Last
    trip, an oil line sprung a leak just above the engine. "Hell
    of a place to be heat-gunning. . . ."

The winch hand rides the greenhorn, who hasn't hit the trap line
    with the hook in four successive tries.

One deck hand's back's gone out.

If the traps are poorly stacked and tied, they'll shift across the
    deck in heavy seas, says the mate. Bone-breakers. Widow-
    makers.

The winch's gears jam. The hands have to haul the traps manually.

The skipper's 22-year-old son is onboard "interning," the old man
    jokes. Problem is, he isn't cutting it.

The cook's working with one hand. Burned the other. It's band-
    aged with a piece of cotton sleeve. He dunks it in cold
    water, sucks the flask.

Sometimes when the fishing is bad, a skipper will go north to the
    lip of the descending ice and drop trap. Hope the gamble
    pays off.

Tonight the temperature with the wind-chill factor is -49°. There's
    weather coming. Waves are sweeping the deck.

The skipper has been at the wheel for 36 hours straight. He unloads on his drag-ass son, misjudges an approach to a trap, has to make the pass again in rolling seas. The greenhorn misses with the hook.

For three weeks the kings have been biting like deerflies. The hold can barely contain them. Sometimes there's no figuring, says the mate. Just sniff the air for crab farts.

The crew place wagers on the number of crabs in the last trap. The greenhorn wins. That's close to a thousand bucks.

Two hands start to wager on whether the harbor will be choked with ice, but the mate won't have it, swears he'll fight them both.

Ironworkers

A murder of crows, they'd have looked like from below,
this clatch of riveters sitting on a girder

eating lunch, 69 floors up, cigarettes,
mugs, thermoses in hand—just a bunch

of guys relaxing. Two of them read the paper,
box scores, handicaps, sitting in the sky

above the sidewalk. One swivels to his right
to light another's smoke. Another roves

along an adjacent beam, as we might pace a
subway platform, except that here a wrong

step would send him, let's not even think
about it. That's the trick, no doubt: Don't stop

to think about it. Any of these guys in peaked
caps and overalls would surely wink

and tell you so: You're eating your buttered roll now.
A little while, you'll go over there and weld

this piece of iron to that. Forget about heights,
winds, contingencies. The only peace

we know is contingent, right? So keep a cool
head, like these Mohawks. You might even grow

to like the elevation, the air, the view. Us,
we're walking iron like you would ride a bike.

Fisher

The fisherman casts
his seine from the dinghy's prow.
A mackerel sky.

Wag

Fandangoing, from bash to bash you go,
deploying whoopie cushions, ersatz vomit,
flogging sleight-of-hand tricks in the foyer,
your sleeve a rabbit hole for wayward face cards.
Winking, you bend your thumb back, double-jointed
as a joy stick. Your prestidigitatory wrist
holds a black belt in hand jive, razzmatazz and hokum
disguised as a Speidel Twist-O-Flex. . . . Spiked punch
sloshes; vanilla crème sandwich cookies
disappear, reappear as chocolate. . . . You're a hoot,
pulling coins from people's ears, palming cards.
But who are you? What's your game? A card yourself
(the Jack of jack?), you're a one-man late-night gag show.
When do you pause for station identification?

Veteran

He carries his
anger with him, a
hip flask in a deep
pocket, periodically
sucking and
staring at nothing
you can see. He's
a dark star, a
nimbus in a peacoat.
Don't accost him:
What he's seen is
what he sees, and
you don't want
to be seen there.

Treasurers

The bottom line: It's not your
father's back office, kemosabe.
Today's corporate treasurer
has more on his plate than
spreadsheets. Spends his day
leveraging networks. Syncing
tranches. Breaking down
internal silos. Tailoring
liquidity solutions to clients'
needs. Integrating foreign
exchange functions and
supply chain finance facilities on,
get this, a single—*uno!*—platform.
Everything's about constructing
win-win situations.
                      Cash and trade
are becoming aligned, you
follow me? Treasurers not only
manage capital and the associated
metrics, they now assemble
digitally enabled toolkits to
manage risk proactively. I'm
telling you, bud, processes,
systems, the whole shebang's
moving away from paper. Cost-
effective? With increased
FX volumes and multiple
convergences, companies have
the option of purchasing their own
receivables!
                Everything's
lateral, baby—no more
top-down. Everything's
real-time and mobile and

insured and cross-insured up the wazoo. . . . Red ink? Gedouttahere! There's a paradigm shift happening, kemosabe.

Copy Editors

A sorry lot of twerps and pseudo-scholars,
aren't they now? And worse! There's clearly some,
how shall we put it, emotional disconnect
going on inside their pencil-pushing souls. . . .
What is one to make of their psychotic argot?
Just listen to them, with their "kills" and "cuts," their
"widows" and "orphans"! Never mind the imputations
of slovenly prose, dangling modifiers, incoherence
they so blithely cast. How about the gall
with which they transpose this and rephrase that?
Like being nibbled to death by ducks! Oh,
you'll see them, lunchtime, with their precious
volumes of poems, their literary biographies.
Snooty bastards! These genteel bloodletters
will carve up a good piece of copy the way a pensioner
whittles a dead branch—not to make something clever
but just to be doing something. And when they say
stet this and *nutshell* that, well, you can bloody well
whiff the attitude a mile away, now can't you?
Copy editors! Where do these fusspot layabouts get off,
mucking with a writer's plainspoken exposition?

Harrier

Isolate maple.
What marathoner brought this
torch to the mountain?

By that burning bush
the trail ascends—into trial.
Runners, take your mark.

Twenty degrees. At
the gun, seasoned harriers
sprint like novices.

The cowpath narrows,
twists, grows suddenly steep. Each
cow his own drover.

Eyes scan the looping
trail for roots, rocks. Overhead:
back-lit bronze and gold.

Downhill straightaway
into the valley of self
mortification.

The final milestone.
A bird whistles from a gulch.
Another answers.

Back on the flats, the
disciplined runner strides. The
driven breaks the tape.

Beyond exhaustion,
satori: The maple's hues
throb. Clouds fly backward.

Poet

for Kristen B.

Forsaking camp, you descend a mile or so
to limn sunset from the Skyline Drive.
Sometimes the autumn sun puts on a show
not even sweetgums and tupelos can contrive
to top: A spectroscopic band of red
glazes the asphalt, travels up the wick
of white line almost to your feet. But ahead
of you is an uphill trek along a leaf-slick
deer run. Time to shake a leg, Shakespeare. . . .
You're hoofing it, scrambling over boles, logs,
in thickening dusk. Off to the side you hear
commotion in the brush. Feral dogs
cross the trail, heads down, nosing a scent.
Not yours, you hope. You're feeling foolish, spent.

Flight Patterns

Flight Patterns

The shadow of a bird, then
the bird. Clouds and the
ghosts of clouds. Scuds
of cirrocumulus dispersed
like popped corn in an
aerial colloid. Below:
parquet of schools, sand lots,
lawns, industrial parks.

Circuit board of cities—
their multihued diodes,
capacitors, transistors; the
ribbons of solder, fine and
reticulate. Slow fade to
snow fields: cirrostratus;
stratocumulus; continents
one could fall through.

Cloud systems like tectonic
plates or glacial masses, the
smaller floes back-lit,
contoured, lambent, the
horizon's titanium yielding
to ultramarine—a tinted
windshield arcing beyond
the jumbo jet's nose cone.

Wherever we were, it's
gone, swallowed up, the
engine's white noise
one with the off-white

broth without. A
play of light and water
through which we move
at several hundred miles an hour.

Our groundling stratagems,
dreamt trajectories,
pissant itineraries—every
pattern we've run or
obsessed about—
scarcely more
substantial
than skywriting.

And the shucked coil? Who
knows? Like adjusting to
progressive lenses? or
no lenses: unpolarized
light, blinding, the
optic fuse blown. . . . The
stewardess understands.
She offers a beverage.

We bank above wooded
suburbs, buzz the big
terrarium whose mossy
turf and watercourses
frame trim inlays of
red-brown, taupe and
ocher quadrilaterals
some call home.

Summons

Yesterday, during a 20-minute lull in the
jackhammering across 121st Street, where
another mega-dormitory is going up, a
songbird—gray with gold markings on its neck—
whistled from my fire escape. What in blazes
was it? What migratory whim or flight
emergency had persuaded it to land in my
back alley, a leafless abyss of brick
walls, cyclone fences, coils of razor wire?
I raised the window and mimicked its call—
a steep Bell curve of a note followed by a
thrice-repeated envoy. Ha! We
went back and forth for a while, me
fine-tuning my whistle with each repetition.
By now the bird was on the highest
rung of the fire escape, bobbing, whistling,
getting wackier by the minute, as if
adjuring my protruding,
Chagallian torso
to follow.

Pheromones

A moth drops a
molecular hankie
and the moon's
eclipsed by gypsy
wings and ashes.

Westhampton Two-Step

The girlfriend gone, the country band disbanded,
I slept, that September, in a dishwasher's backyard
and breakfasted with the want ads. I needed a car,
a crib and, right away, a job. I had stranded
myself without prospects or a game plan
in the Hamptons, where flush missies in chic
sunsuits waft from restaurant to boutique.
One afternoon I lost it: Hoofed, then ran
a couple of miles east along Dune Road,
collapsing on the sand, bellowing at the cloud-
less, chromium sky.
                      Dusk fell. Butterflies
trifled at the edge of the dunes—then began to rise
in legions, a galaxy of orange and black.
I two-stepped that night to the ocean's rhythm track.

Elegy for a Pencil

Sitting on the pot, holding the
book I have to review by tomorrow
open in one hand and the
stub of a pencil in the other, I
begin to underline a phrase when
the pencil scoots out from under my
forefinger, rolls and disappears into the
quarter-inch crack where the tile floor
doesn't quite meet the wall. Double
damn, I say out loud. It's an expression
my father used to use when the simpler
version didn't say enough. I can
see him fuming over his accounts book
or looking for the double-damned
cuff link he'd had in his hands just a
second before or marveling ("I'll
be double-damned . . .") at my
nine-year-old effrontery in putting
his stack of *Reader's Digest*s out
with the trash after he, having
read an article about the dubious
effects of comic books on kids, had
quietly thrown out my collection.
Now I'm wondering what sorry
wonderland of dust balls, plaster
crumbs, roach and mice feces the
damn pencil has gotten itself to. Or
for that matter, what cobwebbed
underworld my father the life insurance
underwriter, dead 17 months now,
has gone to inhabit. ("How long
is this going to take?" he asked,

lucid, during the afternoon of his
last day.) Beyond the halfway
mark myself, I'll find out
soon enough. Meanwhile, I'm
down on my knees and
coming up empty. Deadline
notwithstanding, I've
disappeared like the stub beneath the
floorboards, where anger, grief,
love, fear and guilt persist, dust
bunnies no broom can scatter.

My Father's Pills

The day before my father died, he
began hallucinating. He saw
his pills, loosed from their
opaque bottles, scattered
across his bedsheet and the
floor around his bed. "This
isn't right," he said. "Let's
tidy this up." "Tidy what up?"
my sister asked. "My pills. They're
all over the place." There were no
pills to be seen, we told him, but
he wouldn't buy it. "Look there,"
he said, pointing, "and there, and
there." "No, Dad," we assured him.
Savvy as Gorbachev, he insisted on
independent verification. We
called in my niece. "What do you see
there on the bedsheets?" he asked her.
"Nothing, Grandpa," she said. "This
beats all," he said, tearing up.
                            Was it
the loose ends that were troubling him?
The untidiness of leaving a life behind?
Or the shock of sensing that his world
had drifted so far from ours as to be
unrecognizable?
                The one stone-
cold hallucination I've ever had (I
discount the pulsing colorations of
LSD [Flashback: My dorm room in
1969, a surprise visit by the parents,
my father accidentally knocking over a
brass incense burner containing four
multicolored capsules, my cooking up the

first deliberate lie I'd ever told them, the
generational gulf they'd stopped by to bridge
yawning wider than ever]: This was
no tie-dyed, kaleidoscopic
Disney animation trip but rather a
buzz-saw vision, a shade from hell
ghosting up to claim me) came
when I was recovering from an
appendectomy. On the eighth day,
the nurse gave me my morning
shot of penicillin, and within seconds
a swarm of bees swept through the
open window and attacked me. I
remember the nurse going about her
chores, saying, "No bees in here, uh-uh,
you mus' be dreamin' somethin'. You
dreamin' something?" The terror was
succeeded by an unflappable high, pure
ecstasy of morning. That afternoon, I
told my father about it when he came to visit
on his lunch hour, the August sun making the
most of the room's southern exposure. I
remember him listening, nodding, rustling the
bedsheet in a rippling motion that sent volleys of
breeze across my sweltering legs.
                                        My
hallucination had lasted for 10 or 15
seconds, then subsided. My father's
didn't subside for some time. He saw
the pills as plainly as I had seen the
bees; continued to see them as we
denied they were there. And so
truth became an issue: Was his
family conspiring to hide the truth

from him? Did they think he couldn't
see the pills lying in front of his face?
Was the truth perhaps worse than he
knew? Couldn't his wife and children
bring themselves to level with him?
Or could it be he was actually
losing his marbles? These mutually
heinous possibilities, I'm guessing,
terrified him, though he never
spoke them aloud. (And why
would he? If we were cruel enough
to conspire and lie, what clarification
could he expect? And if we were
treating him like a child out of a
desperate wish to be kind, would he
want to hear the truth plainly spoken?)

Dad's hallucination persisted until he
drifted off for a few hours. He
recalled it when he awoke to say,
with what seemed like frank relief
(though who's to say? which
of us hasn't feigned sleep, satiety,
love, resolve?), Thank God you've
finally stopped fooling around and
tidied up the premises.

Broken Record

for my father, George Christophersen, 1911-2002

I hear you still, life
all but played out—
the needle stuck in the
groove of final passage—
wanting to know "How
long? How long is this
going to take? How long
is this going to take?"
Long enough, Pop,
for you to be broken
on the wheel that
breaks us all.
But in that final
go-round, did the
other vexing questions
continue to swirl? Or
were they subsumed
in the one, as they
were for us who
watched, fearing,
then yearning for,
an end to the
awful spinning?

Veterans Cemetery: Corinth, Miss.

The heat steeps. Scores of katydids
rev collectively, dinning the stalled
air. A hummingbird clears the wall,
hovers beside a crepe myrtle, darts
sideways, arcs, levitates, then—two parts
hornet, one part bird—launches straight
at me, only to stop (bird reincarnate)
on a dime. It vanishes beyond the grid
of headstones.
                    Four p.m. Soon the sun
will dip, then redden like the trumpet vine's
blood-colored bell. The day, suddenly done,
will jack-knife into the Carolina pines
west of town—dusk-gathering trees, wine-
dark, simulating benediction.

Two Men Fighting in a Landscape

The Anxiety of Influence

The critic Harold Bloom coined the phrase
to explain how a writer grows into his trade.
Smitten by a work that outstrips praise,
he copies its effects until he's made
its style his own. For which he feels both guilt
in the borrowing and shame in the kowtowing.
He comes, in time, to resent the borrowed stilt
he's raised himself up by; resolves to fling
the accessory aside, then pauses: What
will he stand on in its stead? His own jack
leg? He has no choice. It's all he's got.
The master's now a monkey on his back,
a burden he must doff. . . . Writer or not,
each of us knows something of this plot.

Anecdote of a Bar

I raced my car to Tennessee,
pulled up at Manco's Bar and Grill.
I washed his deep-fried watercress
down with a gill.

The watercress rose up in a snit,
all acid reflux; roiled around;
pooled on the floor. The room spun round.
(Perhaps the mug of ruby port

had spoiled old Manco's down-home fare?)
My face fluke-belly gray, I bolted
out of there and never gave a hoot
for nothing else in Tennessee.

Ajar in Tennessee

Joshua Bell played violin, once, in a
park underpass in Washington, D.C.
Passersby ignored him. Maybe it was
the sweatshirt and baseball cap—just a
college student busking; not something
worth taking your earbuds out for. Or
maybe the fact that his case wasn't open
threw people off: something askew here,
something odd about the transaction; what's
my role? what does the guy want? Or maybe
context is everything, and emotional response
depends more than we'd care to think upon
social situation, institutional trappings, peer
behavior—visible cues picked up the way
a flock of birds swerves in sync as the
leader banks. One wants to think the poet's
jar—transparent, minimally intrusive, hardly
an object at all, visually speaking, yet something
that occupies, and therefore defines, space; a
figure on a ground where once was slovenly
ground—reorders the Tennessee wilderness
the way, oh, a hornet in a suburban kitchen
alters the feng shui of fruit bowl and marble
countertop (not to mention the human furniture);
wants to think the jar will make the sourwoods
and sweetgums muster up; the Virginia creeper
take on the verve of an art nouveau flourish,
entendriling a landscape jazzed by the see-through
installation. We want our artifacts—hell,
our art—to make a difference; our music
to turn heads, mend steps, override the white

noise, counterpoint the cacophony. But
there he stands, tall and of a port in air,
arpeggios rippling from the bowed strings,
echoing in the park's subterranean chapel,
making everything, and nothing, happen.

Strangers Frightened the Little Chihuahua

for Clifford Hill

One smiled and reeked of queasiness. The other
moved too quickly, yammered inscrutably.
Who could read these galoots? But then,
ditto the Chihuahua, a comic-book pooch
whose raucous yap attested (maintained the
first gent, the other not so sure) to canine
terror masquerading as pugnacity, the way
an overweight cop frisks a gangbanger. There's
still the possibility of amity, trust, the
licking of palms and reciprocal chucking of
jowls tapering off somewhere this side of
shinhump, kissyface and slipperfetch, but first
an apperceptual chasm to be bridged: flash floods
of adrenalin, humors all set to unspool like
antipersonnel devices, slicing and dicing the
ill-fated reconnaissance mission. And so the
Chihuahua yaps, consolidates its personal
space and prerogatives; and the strangers—
leering, toothsome, arms outstretched in the
mixed signals they so blithely employ—
lumber, nattering, toward détente.

Meditation on a Quip by Frost

Free verse, said Robert Frost, is playing
tennis without a net.
The structure gone, what constitutes a
tennis set?

Formal verse, one might reply,
is swimming a regulation
pool with roped-off lanes, versus
an ocean.

To volley just for volley's sake
with no one keeping score
is tennis of a sort. But it can
be a bore.

To swim between lane markers is to
hone a conventional stroke.
To bodysurf a comber is to
go for broke.

A net's an artificial prop—
like racket, ball, court.
An ocean is a natural force,
a poor sport.

Windstorm

for Dave Howard

"I stood right by this window. Stood and stared
as every which way trees started to fall.
That locust? Snapped off, tossed like a knuckleball.
And talk about flukey: Lookit over there,
that wishboned elm? Now look to either side—
everything right as rain. . . . Like a pogo stick,
that wind, I tell you. Touch down, turn its trick,
then jump halfway across the countryside."
"Tornado?" "Might've been, and yet, no black
funnel, as far as I could see. . . . No,
just some loco Connecticut wind, I guess."
"And all the while you stood there keeping track,
Mr. Ed Murrow? You weren't scared? Confess."
"Didn't stop to think—it was that good a show."

Sermon on the Mount

After Reverend's sermon on the Sermon on the Mount,
you said it was only right I drop by and see
about his mount—the chestnut filly he'd bought
from your brother in May; the quarter horse that straightaway
came down with worms, a twice-recurring rash
and a crocodile's temper, to hear the Reverend tell it
("The stiff-necked creature kicked her stall to pieces").
Says your brother later, swearing up and down,
"These preachers toil not, neither do they ken."

The Reverend, proud of his manse, walked me around
the property, the garden; gestured at the yield;
pointed, winking, to his "lillies of the field";
then owned that the quarter horse had gentled down
some since May, and would make a pretty thing.
From the rise, where he'd fenced and staked tomato plants,
we watched the filly grazing by the barn—
then saw her shake her head and snort and shy,
a plume of hornets ghosting from the ground,

strafing her face, her milk-and-whisky eyes.
She raced across the pasture, bucking twice
at the north fence, then veered and galloped back,
the scarf of hornets trailing from her flank;
pulled up and fell to spinning in her tracks.
Later, as we hosed the creature's back,
neck and sides—whose welts, the Reverend marveled,
put him in mind of the rash she'd had in May—
the mystery of the splintered stall came clear.

This chestnut is an even-tempered horse:
I have your brother's sober oath for that.
What happened, mark my word, is these damned hornets
with their nest beneath the barn, got all het up

and swarmed the quarter horse inside her stall. . . .
The Reverend had no kerosene. "How's that?" I said.
He scratched a tuft of whiskers, then: "Praise God,"
he boomed as if a congregation stood before us.
"Praise God, who gave them tougher hides than ours."

The nearest kerosene was at your brother's—
who was in his cups, as usual, when I arrived
and told what happened. I got the wonted earful
about how our good shepherd had a thing or two to learn
about raising horses. Then your brother puts his glass down,
snorts, tilts his chair against the kitchen wall
and cracks his knuckles: "My counsel for the Reverend,
bless his purblind soul and sensitive hide:
Consider the fillies of the field. 'Provide, provide.'"

Composed Upon the George Washington Bridge

Earth has not anything so damned unfair
as a traffic tie-up on a major artery
into Manhattan after a summer holiday—
Independence Day, for instance. Spare
me the stench of diesel fumes. Spare
me the car and bus exhaust; the 90-degree
heat; the bass line pulsing from the SUV
with the sound-stage speakers; the distant flare
portending some multivehicle fatality;
the sense that *my* lane in particular is going nowhere
fast; the gradually increasing need to pee;
and every other trial that attends reentry
into the City We Just Fled. Good God! Isn't there
some other way to pay the piper's fee?

An Essay on Pope

You make a cogent case, I must admit,
For cleaving to beliefs that scarcely fit
The modern world. Your logic is a blade
That dices prettily, but can't persuade.
You champion the status quo and rate
The churl who would improve his sorry state;
Invoke fine phrases—each a golden calf
That, even with fresh paint, won't fool by half.
"Great Nature spoke. . ."? And would that be the wasp,
The scorpion, the earwig or the asp?
"Nature's law"? Blood, clotting in the dirt;
The fierce eating the frail for dessert.
"Reason"? What we use to extenuate
The deeds that conscience otherwise would hate.
"Order is Heaven's law"? I guess its dearth
Hereabouts just goes to show *we* live on *Earth*.
"Great chain of being"? A basketball-league ranking:
Big teams on top; smaller contenders tanking.
Well-tempered cosmos? "Music of the spheres"?
Must be the Big Bang ringing in his ears. . . .
"One truth [say what?]: Whatever is, is right"?
Memo to Mr. Pope: Go fly a kite.

In the Pines

after James Tate

Our ploy a whiz-bang *fait accompli*,
we stole through the foliage like bureaucrats on leave,
now trundling, now embracing among the lichens.
Reflexive premonitions outflanked my composure, but
you, my Duck, were a smash, stuttering in all the right places,
ruminating conspicuously like a mortified friar, lofting
hallelujahs *sotto voce*, as we slid down the lip of the carapace.
A bout of peace and quiet ensued. Loblollies
whittled conical gewgaws in the air above our heads.
"Don't ever welch on me, my Larkspur," I said,
keeping a light rain on my emotions, "or
the synergy we siphoned off may put to rout
this perfect dusk where grackles call and
ambulences veer along a ribbon of highway. . . . Hush:
What's that song in my heart, whose melody
fluctuates in the valley? It's name, which I know so well,
hully-gullies on the palate of my tongue, my Rose,
my Ruse, my Garden Hose, my Rosicrucian, and now
I burn with unrequited nostalgia. If only we'd
listened when they announced the night's agenda,
when the grounds crew rolled up the carpet of needles and
the carpetbaggers fled with their ill-gotten gains, but
we didn't, and now my beeper beeps not-so-sweet remorse."

A Malediction for Bidding, "'Morning!"

As exhausted athletes sleep away,
dreaming of three-point jumpers drained,
passes intercepted, double-play
balls scooped, home court advantages gained,

so do I love to sleep: through dawn
and breakfast summons, first alarm
and "snooze." My shade's invariably drawn.
My head is lolling on my arm

and means to loll the morning through:
I'm catching zzz's till noon or one,
one-thirty, one-forty-five, two.
I like to sleep, Jack, till I'm done.

A sleeping man is such a thing
as an antipersonnel device:
Wise men pause before venturing
to approach; tiptoe by like mice.

Sleep's a sort of chimney sweep
scouring the brain's besmuttered flue;
a toilet plunger that will keep
Mind's toilet functioning good as new.

An automobile mechanic's truck,
it tows us out of emotional ruts;
night's grease monkey, it tries its luck
at bracing the psyche's overtaxed struts.

A good sleep, like a tweezers, plucks
unruly thoughts from the inner brow
and, like a velvet pitchfork, mucks
the decks of Ego's garbage scow.

So don't come piping round my door
with your hale and hearty "Rise-and-shine!"
and "Up-and-at-'em!" and "Sleep-no-more!"
A pox upon your vertical spine!

Off the Fashion Police

for William Matthews

The pigeon's green-mauve-orange-coral-gray
should turn our stomachs—such a color clash!
Nature, though, is nothing if not brash.
And culture is a mishmash. Who's to say
what matches what? which combination works?
why this much repetition makes us dance
and that much makes us drowsy? In Provence,
a poetry of elaborate formal quirks
was counted sexy—the troubadours' bees' knees.
Shell-encrusted gewgaws once made queens
swoon. Sketches of industrial machines
inspired Miro's color symphonies.
Fashion laughs at any litmus test
but one: Whatever lasts, laughs best.

For Galway Kinnell   (1927–2014)

1

You knew as well as anyone the bitch was
gone in the teeth. You celebrated her eyes.

2

Celebratory verse comes slow to my hand. Much as I love
"The Avenue Bearing the Initial of Christ into the New World,"
my muse is Germanic: Think "The Wanderer," "The Seafarer"—
Anglo-Saxon elegies whose charred ruins, hagridden exiles,
tribal codes and *ubi sunts* make them this Bronx refugee's
wry touchstones. Yet, like you, I came to love at least a slice
of Avenue C, part of a 'hood so run-down and forgotten, a
bar that booked bluegrass musicians was able to hang on for a
decade beyond the millennium, following its retro bent long after
commercial rents on First had jumped several orbitals and
the "charming, prewar" firetraps on Avenue A had gone co-op.
"9C"—the doggery on the corner of 9th: Where the likes of the
Rock-House Gamblers retailed Stanley Brothers ballads and the
death of Jimmy Martin was commemorated by an ad hoc free
concert featuring nationally known talent, whose manic fans
spilled onto the sidewalk, where latecomers stewed and settled
for whatever they could hear filtering through a half-open door.
9C—a dive surrounded by century-old tenements, liquor stores,
mom & pop bodegas, crack dens, chop shops & the odd itinerant
snow cone vendor, roasted nuts peddler or peeled-orange hustler.
Whose urban mandolinists and banjo pickers, inured to boom-box
salsa, would warm up across the street in a rubble-lot-cum-
community-garden, its cyclone fence symmetrically festooned
with sculptures made of junked phones, welded utensils, soda

cans, plastic dolls, umbrella struts and tinted bottles; a lot whose
scant half acre was planted in, or colonized by, ferns, mimosas,
berry bushes, green beans, fulvous herbs, viney nondescripts and
weedy what-alls—foliage you'd want to hack with a machete, so
dense and tendriled was the life foliating there. . . .

Which, of course, is what your poem delineates—
the cheek-by-jowl, hodgepodge *mishegas*
of Avenue C, aorta of America.

3

Which never was the City on a Hill
it fancied itself, but a city of the plain
blessed with a first-rate harbor: a commercial
port with an outperforming public
relations department, whose promotional brochures
and slogans were so ennobling, we bought them.
But having bought them, eventually unwrapped them:
held them to the nose to see what we had got.
Bloodied during a voter registration
drive in Louisiana, you caught a whiff
of something noisome—not as advertised.
"The promise was broken too freely," is how you put it
in your poem on Avenue C. "*Oy weih, oy weih.*"

4

I met you once, in 1973.
A fledgling wage earner and musician, I was
subletting a saltbox in Wainscot, a community of

potato farms sandwiched between the Hamptons on
Long Island's froufrou, stinking-rich South Fork.
You knocked on the door in your red and black
woodsman's shirt late one October afternoon, as an
ocean breeze made the willow in the yard sway and
shimmer. You had come to see Nate, the lessee.
He's gone to the city, I said. Who shall I tell him called?
Galway Kinnell, you said.
The poet? I asked.
Yes, you said.
I . . . write a bit myself, I said,
but my poems are rubbish.
That's good, you said. Don't
throw them out. A bad poem
is the larval stage of a good poem.

I wish I had that moment back.
I should have sent you off with an armload of newly chopped
kindling, some windfall Bartletts from the orchard,
a bag of cauliflower from the garden out back—some
token of thanks for such astute, uncondescending words.
I'll tell Nathaniel you came by, I said. So long, you said,
walking back to your Schwinn with the jury-rigged basket.

Confections of a Hooligan

for Kenneth Koch

Who are you calling a field?
This corncrake is a blue jar
and you, a scandal unfurling behind its beveled maw.

* * *

Provincial ennui stalks Isaiah's cow.
O, country of terrible foods!
The calving tongue glistens in the nettles.

* * *

Not for nothing have the whelps raked the footpath.
I gallop on, brooding like a woodpecker on a turntable.

* * *

My brutish poems feed on sadness and marionettes.
Silver-plated futtocks brace the kite.
On the blue steppes: the nightclub of spleen.

* * *

Bully for October! The cupcake's
in the corncrake, where a choir screams
and strives fitfully to excel.

* * *

The cities light up like lepers at Seder.
I'm not a canary. Yet I am ready
with a pure heart to wear my sweater.

* * *

I have loved, sometimes, to munch on earth
and sally forth among rapscallions.
But sin infiltrates the flimsiest loam.
Yesterday's loaves? They're toast.

* * *

Why this wheat field of souls departing?
I ply my grandma's misanthropic limb
as wry tinkers cry "Great Neck."

* * *

Say what? A clod's belaboring the pasta!
Single parents fume and snort. What
solvent fellow is smirking in the corncrake?

* * *

You did not know I had
drubbed a thick bloke with a
smattering of brass earrings.
Now I earn a different wage.
I raise the glass and
remember your sorry fatigues.

The Bee-Loud Glade

1
I have stood there, frozen in place—
the meadow a minefield of vespiaries, the lilac
air a skein of flight paths.

2
The bean rows are approachable, but
the garden drones like an engine.
At the dog's misstep, a swirling
plume ghosts from the ground:
a scarf that won't be doffed.

3
The cabin? Walls, wattled eaves
shagged with paper cones, daubed
excrescences. I lift the latch,
face and shoulders flinching. Come,
night, come rain and freezing weather.

4
I came to cultivate solitude; to
attend to growing things.
But the beans keep their own counsel;
the solitude's sprouted wings.
I thought to circumvent the world
of clerks and clocks and wives—
but go about distracted by the
buzz of nest and hive.

5
I should arise and go now, but
something roots me here:
paralysis of purpose? striped
chemistry of fear?

No oracle but this hornet's nest
whose dark eye stares me down.
A poet is a fool. I'll
take my chances in the town.

God Has 99 Names (and an Unlisted Number)

1

Oh stop. The kneeling supplicant! Like you,
I've stuffed my rolled-up prayers into a bottle,
flung it from a cliff, then watched it drop
and disappear in the chameleon blue;
gone home, undaunted, and—behold, the true
believer!—penned another SOS
bound for the same inscrutable address
as the last. The lost. Dead letter. Toodaloo.
Don't gape at me as if I were depraved!
Delusionary obsession—that's the name
of this hapless game.ABuse me pro gasp
equals Belief. It seems we can't sit still
for oblivion, so we cultivate the flame
of faith: *This one will find Him; I'll be saved.*

2

"I want, I want. . . ." This isn't Disneyland.
Give me this and that, the toddler says.
You don't want God; you want a personalized Pez
dispenser serving candy on demand!
"The world's a roiling snake pit; God's to blame."
Yes, a snake pit. And a contradance,
malaria, a seventh-grade romance,
wasps, a watercolor without a frame. . . .
A smithereen of star persists; life
wriggles from a percolating sump.
Organic chemistry. *Miracle, all the same.*
And subject to chance and flux, mutation, strife. . . .
Why choose to picture God as Home Plate Ump
missing calls? Suck it up; play the game.

The Take-Away

M. was crouching in a hole when
something whined close by, and
off to his left, J.'s mooncalf face
imploded. "Good God," M. whispered
preposterously. Then something
whined still closer. He woke up
in the medics' tent, screaming.
After the third shot of morphine, he
learned his leg was gone. "No," he said,
"don't mess with me like that. That's
not right." Next day he tried to
throttle the medic, but the brawny
medic pinned his shoulders to the cot.
"Listen, bud," he said, "here's the deal:
You're alive and a hundred other guys
are dead. Get it?" It took three nights,
but he got it. "Thank God," M. said,
repeating it in the dark like a mantra.
A few days later, after the medic had
changed the dressing and he'd got done
screaming, he asked the medic to
put him down. "Just make a mistake
with the dosage, huh? Anybody can make
a mistake, you know? *Do this for me?*"
Later he tried to rip the bandages off, and
the medics applied restraints. Stateside, a
"hero" rehabbing in the vet hospital, he stopped
talking. What was the point?
                          Occasionally,
though, he spoke to God. What he said
wasn't always abusive. There were
moments when banked coals blazed and

a manic sense of gratitude made his
eyes tear up. His prayerful communiqués,
he realized, were incoherent.
                                      Months passed.
When he let himself think, he thought
about all kinds of things: knot-tying,
pole-vaulting, the ant kingdom, the way
ants shrivel under a magnifying glass.
One day he thought about Jacob. Not
his dead buddy (well, him too, how
not to?), but the Biblical Jacob, who
wrestled with God, and whose
leg God, that wily streetfighter,
dislocated at the hip, pulling
thigh bone from ball joint, crippling
Jacob because he wouldn't yield.
Jacob, whose modus operandi was
holding on tight (hadn't he been born
grasping his twin brother's ankle?)
and eventually prevailing, had
wrangled with God for a blessing.
Presumptuous puts it mildly. A
sort of gung-ho chutzpah. . . .

The only blessing M. had ever asked for
had been to live through that harrowing
night. And he had—at least part of him
had. Had lived, that is, to know the pain
of other harrowing nights, nights
that were even worse than cringing in a
hole and getting shot at.

Jacob's life too, M. recalled, had been
spoiled early. He'd been conned out of
seven years' labor by his uncle, Laban, whose
bait-and-switch bride scam and wage manipulations
the young, dependent nephew had had to sit still for. . . .
Maybe that's neither here nor there. But
to ask a blessing presupposes a God who
intervenes, who's actively involved—a God
who therefore bears at least some smidgen of
responsibility for raw deals, rampant wrongs.
Jacob's predisposition aside, did some such
gut-level assumption lie behind his limpet
tenacity? Exploited for years, how
resentful had he become? Now, headed home,
he wants a blessing, and he's going to have it,
even if he has to wrest it from God's throat. . . .

And *he prevails*. He even receives a name that
celebrates his having fought God to a standstill.
An honorific name . . . A crippled leg . . . *What's
the take-away here? Is the fool's errand
of contending with God self-defeating?
game-changing? both? I'm holding on, but
Hey: I need to know the take-away here.*

Two Men Fighting in a Landscape

A doughboy and a Tory exchange blows.
To the right, at the edge of the moor, a brook
glints like shod hooves on cobblestones as
dawn breaks through a gap in the cloud cover.
The warriors huff and fume; the sound
of the brook is the sound of a galaxy swarming.

Dawn steeps. Atomized droplets
emulsify the countryside.
Vegetable matter everywhere plucks up.
A bird goes off: like a radio.
The men continue sparring, as the
cobalt sky gives way to lighter cobalt.

The Wanderer

The Wanderer

translated from the Anglo-Saxon

Who ships alone may live to inherit
mercy, though his soul sound the deep;
though he weather gales, griefs; ply
an exile's oar in a hoary sea.
Fate teaches even as it tasks.

—Thus the vagabond, wracked with cares,
remembering his mangled kin:
"Alone at dawn, I long to speak
my heart, but no one now is left
to whom I dare lay bare this woeful
screed. Besides, I see full well
the need for keeping cares and trials
locked in the breast, bound fast
in soul's strongbox, subject to will.
A broken spirit won't stand against Wyrd;
a craven brow brings nothing about.
The warrior buries blood-yearnings
in the vault of an undaunted heart.
  "And so, all soul-stirrings of home,
wraiths of kinsfolk killed—I've tried
to tie them fast; to fetter them;
to bury them as I buried my lord
and liege, who gave me golden torques.
Sightless, I covered his corpse with earth;
fled far from that fearful place;
crossed waters, clashing currents; sought
some new dispenser of pelf and favor
well away—some wine- or mead-hall
by whose hearth a hapless wretch
might hope to sleep and serve a king
inclined to comfort and claim him, open-
handed.

"He who has had to wander
alone and unknown knows how harsh
a cohort care can be; how hard,
to set forth seconded by ghosts.
Exile's rigors rake his path.
No gold's bestowed to gladden his heart.
Instead of torques, a torquing cold
cramps his ribs as he calls to mind
bold retainers, times of hoard-sharing,
how as a youth he used to be welcome
at the board of a king. That's behind him now.
  "The man who makes his way without
the counsels of a beloved king
soon learns that sorrow and sleepless nights
dull the wits. The warrior dreams
he wraps his arms around his warlord's
legs, embraces him as in bygone days,
head listing on his lordship's knee
as it did when he sat in the seat of grace. . . .
Jarred, he snaps to his senses, glimpses
combers, eyes the yellow surge where
sea-birds bob, splaying their feathers.
Snow swirls. Sleet chases hail.
  "The wanderer's heart heaves again.
Harbored griefs gather anew.
Beloved kinsmen hover above
the waves; float on the foam, saying nothing.
He calls to his friends, cups his hands.
They flit away. . . . The weary soul,
sent out beyond those breakers once
too often, stops struggling back.

         "At times I see no reason why
a man, on sounding mankind's plight,
does not lose hope. Behold the earl,
called without warning to quit the floor
of his hall forever. And never a day
goes by but some thane somewhere falls.
Yet none grows wise but weathers his share
of winters. The seasoned warrior bides
his time; speaks not in temper or haste;
neither hangs back nor hies ahead of the field;
doesn't cringe or clown or covet gold;
boasts no more than is mete and right;
keeps his peace till experience prompts
and he knows full well which way the tides
of a swollen heart may surge or shift.
         "The staid warrior understands that wealth
is sand. Not every earthen wall
harrowed by blizzards is built to stand
the onslaught, nor every eave the snow.
Wine-halls crumble; kings die,
cut off from their dreams; cohorts perish
beside their walls. War carries off some
beyond recall. One is borne away
by a bird-ghoul over billowing seas;
Death and wolves dispatch another.
A butchered earl is squirreled away
in an earthen trench by a taut-faced squire.
         "Likewise the Maker laid waste the mounds
of the old ones; made bold clamors cease.
The strongholds of the giants stand idle now.
The wise man will weigh the lessons
of this wall-stead; of this woeful life,

these remote slaughters; will stop and ask:
'Where is the war-horse? the warrior's son?
the hoard-sharer, his hand ever open?
the banquet-seat? What's become of the roistering
mead-hall? the burnished mugs? the lusty
men clad in coats of mail?'
So much for a prince: Past glories
go black beneath the helm of night.
Towering walls wrought with torqued
snake shapes stand athwart
the footpaths of a fallen cordon.
The ashen spear, unsated by slaughter:
How many earls has it unmade!
Storms beset stone bulwarks.
Snow and frost fetter the ground—
winter's herald, hedged by a creeping
shadow: night's unwelcome shade.
Blizzards bury what man has made.
Nothing but miseries for middle earth,
as Wyrd remakes the world under heaven.
Here wealth is fleeting, friends are fleeting,
man is fleeting, woman is fleeting.
Our dwelling-place too will turn to dust."

 —So the wise man sits apart; takes soundings of his fate;
cleaves, meanwhile, to his faith; is ever loath to loose
the ire that roils his breast till he fathom how best to use it.
An earl endures his lot. Blessed is he who seeks mercy
and solace from the heavenly Father, in whom we all stand fast.

Notes

"Bishop's Crook Lamppost": The Giants played baseball in New York before moving to San Francisco. The Five Satins: a black doo-wop group popular in the mid-1950s.

"Grandma and Grandpa T. in a Prospect of Flowers": Charles Van Doren, a long-reigning champion on the TV quiz show "Twenty One," later confessed before Congress to having received the questions beforehand.

"Copy Editors": "Widows," "orphans"—In copy editors' argot, a widow is a column line containing only one word, the last in a paragraph. An orphan is a first line of a paragraph stranded at the bottom of a column. This poem is dedicated to my colleagues in the trade.

"Ajar in Tennessee": See Wallace Stevens' "Anecdote of the Jar."

"Confections of a Hooligan": Overtired, I kept misreading lines in Sergei Esenin's *Confessions of a Hooligan*. Some of the misreadings generated this poem. It is dedicated to my college professor and adviser, Kenneth Koch, who spirited American poetry out of the ivory tower into the playground.

"For Galway Kinnell": *ubi sunt* (Lat.): Where are they now?

"The Wanderer": "Wyrd" (l.15)—Anglo-Saxon: destiny. I've looked to preserve the Anglo-Saxon conventions of the original poem, rendering the accentual patterns of alliteration found in Old English verse. I have tried, as well, to use words deriving from Anglo-Saxon, wherever possible. I venture a fresh reading of the poem's fifth line, a gateway gnome that is commonly rendered, "Fate is inexorable" (S.A.J. Bradley, *Anglo-Saxon Poetry*), or "Fate is inflexible" (Kevin Crossley-

Holland, *The Anglo-Saxon World: An Anthology*). That reading is not only tautological: It subverts the thrust of the poem—the speaker's progressive understanding that experience can educate (and perhaps even afford input into our destinies?). The interpretive challenge lies in *arǣd,* the line's operative word. In a glossary entry in *Seven Old English Poems*, the scholar John C. Pope defines it as "determined, inexorable," but says: "The word is not very well attested. . . . Perhaps a shortened form of *arǣded.* See *rǣdan.*" The entry for *rǣdan* opens a new window of interpretation. Its meaning, "give counsel, instruct," is the one I opt for.

About the Author

Bill Christophersen was born and raised in the Bronx. He attended Columbia University, where he studied poetry with Kenneth Koch, Jill Hoffman and David Shapiro and received a Ph.D. in American literature. His poems have won awards from *Kansas Quarterly* and *The Robinson Jeffers Tor House Foundation* and been nominated several times for a Pushcart Prize, as well as for inclusion in *Best New Poets*. His book reviews and critical essays on poetry have appeared in *Newsweek*, *The New York Times Book Review*, *The American Book Review*, *Poetry, Shenandoah* and elsewhere. The author of *The Apparition in the Glass: Charles Brockden Brown's American Gothic* (University of Georgia Press), he lives and works in New York and plays traditional and bluegrass fiddle.